ABOUT LUNAR POETRY PODCASTS

Lunar Poetry Podcasts was founded by David Turner in October 2014 in Camberwell, South London (just 'round the corner from Arment's Pie & Mash) as a series of three long-form interviews uploaded to YouTube. Since then it has grown into an archive of discussions, interviews and recordings with 230+ poets and spoken word artists from around the world. The series has been shortlisted in both the Saboteur Awards and British Podcast Awards and is now archived by the British Library.

David Turner is the founding editor of the Lunar Poetry Podcasts series, has a City & Guilds certificate in Bench Joinery along with the accompanying scars, is known to the Southwark Community Mental Health Team as a 'service user' and has represented Norway in snow sculpting competitions. Originally from London but now living in Bristol. Widely unpublished. Working-class. Picket line poet.

'Why Poetry?'

The Lunar Poetry Podcasts Anthology

VERVE
POETRY PRESS
BIRMINGHAM

PUBLISHED BY VERVE POETRY PRESS
Birmingham, West Midlands, UK
https://vervepoetrypress.com
mail@vervepoetrypress.com

FIRST PUBLISHED SEP 2018

Printed in the UK by TJ International

Cover image *I Fall Where You Weave* (glass, Icelandic grass, 2017)
by Carissa Baktay, photographed by D10 PHOTO.

ISBN: 978-1-912565-09-2

This book is dedicated to Alex Goddard,
one of the earliest supporters of
jacking in the joinery in favour of
pissing about with poetry.
Her absence is keenly felt.

CONTENTS

FOREWORD

This is a distillation of Lunar Poetry Podcasts, in its purest form.

If you are new to Lunar, you may be mistaken in thinking it's a podcast about poems. It would be more accurate to call it a podcast about poets. It's interested in who we are, what we do, and how our personal experience of being a body in the world shapes the relationship with what we write or perform.

Each episode has been the start of a conversation that needed to happen. Some have been about process, about ripping poems from skulls and mashing them into substance. Some have been niche: interdisciplinary approaches to the concept of 'rest' (Episode 62, 'Rest'); poets who write theatre in West Yorkshire (Episode 98, 'Poetry & theatre-making in West Yorkshire'); or the translation of one man's *Attempt at Exhausting A Place in Paris* into a collaborative experiment in East London (Episode 46, 'Collaboration'). Many, many of the conversations have been vital. We'll explore more of those in a moment.

Recently, David told me that he initially wanted the podcast to feel like a zine. Maybe this is the most accurate depiction of what Lunar has become. It's free, easy to access, and provides a whole collage of voices, in a medley of different forms. It could be read as a series of manifestos, piling perspective on perspective, idea on idea. It's exciting to listen to, because it doesn't offer easy answers or homogenous voices. Where else would you find Giles L. Turnbull alongside Travis Alabanza and Mary Jean Chan?

As with all effective manifestos, Lunar shows by doing. When he wanted to make a point about how Arts Council funding can and should be spent, David went ahead and published the series' statistics. He has openly posted reports, not only of Lunar's achievements, but of the things he's learned and things he'd like to do better. Where episodes have focused on the experience of writers from marginalised communities, Lunar has repeatedly handed its platform over completely to the members from the community in question, whilst emphasising that experiences are personal, and one person's voice does not speak for all.

As a disabled writer, who doesn't often get to leave the house, I've learned more about access to the arts by taking part in a single 60-minute episode, than through 29 years of living on this planet (Episode 89, 'Accessibility in the Arts'). And long after the interview ended, I still feel like part of the conversation. Discussion has extended onto social media, affecting the way I work and think. The podcast has travelled, bringing me poets and poems from all over the UK and beyond. Transcripts have been added, offering alternative ways to engage.

And now, the podcast has evolved even further, into this solid little book. If you are wondering why such a range of ways to interact is important, I would invite you to consider again the range of experiences Lunar shares. In Episode 57 two poets identifying as QTIPOC discuss how being read or perceived as 'aggressive' might affect a performance (Episode 57, 'Black QTIPOC'). A conversation with Freedom News turns to the need for people in prison to have access to physical paper (Episode 37, 'Freedom News'). Time and time again, the podcast illustrates how vital it is to consider the contexts in which poetry is being made, used and explored.

Many of the poems in the book are new. Most of them have never even featured on the podcast. I believe this is fitting. If this book is a distillation of Lunar, it was bound to stimulate new ideas. But consider, too, the gaps between the poems: extracts of discussions from the podcast, where writers talk about the aspects of the writing process which are most important to them. Notice that the weight of the words is almost equal between ideas about what it means to make a poem, and the poetry itself.

Equally fitting is a vein which runs throughout the anthology, where I finally get to turn the tables and interview David Turner. It's highly edited (as two pretty notorious talkers, our original discussion ran to over 13,000 words). But, like the book itself, I like to think of our edit as a distillation - the essence of David and his manifesto for creating a poetry podcast series. It's important to hear him talk about what it means to be host, producer and editor, in a podcast that aims for representation over diversity. Interviewing David has offered me a new respect for what he's learned to do: just stop talking and listen for a moment.

Abi Palmer
2018

'Why Poetry?'

Introduction – Part One

Abi Palmer: Let's start at the beginning. When you first began Lunar Poetry Podcasts, what were you looking to achieve?

David Turner: So, back in the spring of 2014, I first read at a poetry open-mic night at The Dragon Cafe, a mental-health support group. Then the following week, I read at the legendary Poetry Unplugged, currently hosted by Niall O'Sullivan. Between then and the summer, I started attending as many open-mic nights and poetry events as I could... I was just desperate to know more.

I wanted to know why people kept coming to these nights. I felt like at every poetry event, there were at least two people I was desperate to talk to. I wanted to ask them these questions: things I was wondering, and I didn't know enough about poetry, so there were gaps in my knowledge.

Early on I met Sean Wai Keung and Anna Kahn. They were probably the first actual poets to come and talk to me at an open-mic. Once I'd befriended a few poets, we started gathering... I don't think either of those two smoke, but I have this image in my mind of people huddling outside poetry events, smoking, having these conversations.

Once I started being invited into conversations, I just thought it was ridiculous if other people didn't get to share. There are so many people that can't access conversations like this, and I wanted them to be as public and accessible as possible. And the slightly more selfish thing about it was that, if I started this project, I could get poets to myself for a couple of hours and bombard them with questions.

On the podcast, you talk very openly about coming from a working-class background, and also your experience of mental illness. Did either of these experiences have an impact on your own access to the arts?

I'm lucky that I come from a household where both my parents read a lot, mainly romance and horror novels, so I was surrounded by books. It goes back to the idea that just because you identify in some way, your personal experience will still be different to others that identify in the same way. Whilst it's valid and true that for some working-class people, the only reading material was a newspaper on a Sunday, that's not always the case...

Just because you're working class, it doesn't mean in any way you're unable to engage with the arts. What it might mean is that you engage with a very particular type of the arts. The same could be said of middle class and beyond. But being working class, I did encounter a stereotype that poetry is trying to be too clever. If you are into poetry, you're trying to be too clever, and that is seen as aspirational which can be really poisonous when identifying as working class.

I failed my English Literature GCSE and went on from school to serve a joinery apprenticeship. For three months, I did half of a Fine Art foundation course. I broke my elbow falling off a scaffold and couldn't finish, but I was offered places at Wimbledon School of Art, to study sculpture, and Goldsmiths to read History of Art. But I turned those things down.

The reason I failed my English GCSE and didn't go to university is because, both times, I was having borderline emotional breakdowns. That's how my mental illness has impacted the way I interact with the arts. It has physically stopped me interacting with life, and by extension, the arts.

My mental health, specifically for me bipolar type 2, has incapacitated me at times, has disabled me physically and mentally and emotionally for obscenely long stretches of my life. It stopped me engaging with anything, never mind the arts.

When did you start thinking about poetry again?

I wrote a lot in my late teens and early 20s. Then I had a really severe emotional breakdown. I suppose I was about 24. It was the first time I ended up in hospital. It was only a short stay but it was a big thing to happen.

I stopped writing at that point. I didn't write again until I was 33. The spring of 2014, I was admitted to the Maudsley psychiatric hospital in South London and I spent five weeks there. In there, I was encouraged to write. I had issues with compulsive and intrusive thoughts and I was encouraged to write these down because I couldn't articulate them at the time. I've never really had any problem talking about my mental health, but at that time, I was emotionally exhausted and couldn't articulate. So I was encouraged to write these things down and when I left, I had these notebooks of lists, of phrases and sentences, which looked like poems but didn't read as poems.

At that time, I felt like they were poems that didn't function. This is one of the things about this being a journey, or an education, for me in poetry. I now know that they are found poems, and list poems. I didn't know that at the time. I didn't know what these things were that I was writing. [...]

Canada
Helen Mort

back country   your country
tracks dividing powder slopes
height I swallowed til it burned
my throat   I turned
the ice blue lake and sentry trees
could never keep me upright

all night   outside
cougars bears and wolverines
paced silently beneath
the Highway caught
on cameras at the crossing points
their bodies x-ray flickers

pale   as the the bad photograph
of your trapper girlfriend
I could hardly see   her shape
my outline in the Bow Summit
snow again   again
the landscape printing me

or the husky   too dumb to teach
stilled by a metal chain
his fur the Whitehorse winter
you were running from
three days walking   no sleep
up to your waist in it

this dream   I get
about a north I've never seen
the sky a static screen
and the cabins unlit
you wouldn't like it there
you said

and my silence   folded
like the shut wings of a raven
on the bonnet of your car
the opposite of ghost
shaking every empty thing
picking the rubber tip

of an ice screw hammering
your roof rack   a girl
in a footballer's hotel room
the week after   week before
that moaned phrase   the nape
of her neck   a locked door

like that   the way
you look at me
the skyline on the Icefields
Parkway   pleated rock
all bunched and gathered up
and you say some routes are safe

tell me   a story
how you left and where you built
your new place while America
ruins itself all night
on television   and out there
mountains are castles without kings

tell me   everything
I'm listening except
when you touch me
then I'm on the Greyhound bus
from Jasper two years ago
a black bear vanishing in woods

before dawn   a man
will walk across the Prairie
name each plant and gift them
with a cure   bark
for hair loss   juniper
for memory   heather

for the changing cells inside me
you touch them too
this large scale map
Kam Loops   Medicine Hat
I want to move here I said
and never moved

Episode 03 – December 2014

Helen Mort: *A lot of my beginnings for poems do come from sound, almost like an ear worm or something. Often, I'll be doing something else, walking or maybe running. I'll get this thing in my head and have to sort of run the lines over and over until I settle into a pattern. It is almost as if I can see them in my mind's eye, slotting into place, a bit like 'Tetris'. I'll often not write it down for a long time, I repeat the lines over and over in the hope that when I do finally come to write it down, I'll have forgotten the weaker stuff. It's terrible, when you're at an event and there's lots of people around, [thinking] "I just need to write this line or I'm going to forget it". So, often it's quite a stressful process.*

content
Sean Wai Keung

sitting in my bedsit + with no money left
it becomes harder to not think about the past
even though its a sin to think about the past
even though nothing good comes
from thinking about the past

but i cant go outside as outside is full
of temptation to spend - a constant
reminder of the horribleness of now not
like in the past when things were different
in the past when leaving was still an option

in the past when i had no money things always
turned out ok eventually but thats not like now -
i feel that this communication may be my last -
that i may not survive this month + that all
people will remember of me is this place

so please remember for when it does all finally end
that i hated everything about this part of my life
no matter how many poems i may have written about it

please tell everyone that i never bothered fighting
until the end - that instead i accepted my fate
with a smile on my face + no remorse

after all ive already paid my rent for this month
i may as well spend the rest
of my time here doing
greater things

Episode 06 – February 2015

David Turner: *Why does [poetry] suit what you want to say or communicate?*

Sean Wai Keung: *Because it's open to play, not just with message or content or image, but also with form. You can play with images, you can play with expectations, you can play with the sounds of words and the rhythm of words. I've always enjoyed rhythmical things so that's why it suits me.*

And what's in yours?

Lizzy Turner

What frightens me is
I can't see exactly
what's stuck on the
inside of my body,
what, alongside coffee staining,
bad thought never quite sloughed,
curdling on a raw wall,
what might interrupt my
blood at a later date,
something sitting in there,
a gristle rock,
no memory of mine
but with its own,
haunted little misery of a thing,

I'm scared to think
inside of my body,
feel from the surface
quiet bumps which don't
reveal the features underneath,
what event made my
waist bend in like this?
pulled me together and
where did it go?
I think of how the
things get in and get
transported through the system,

I fear the poisons which
won't leave the body fully,
clawmarks in the padding
round the exits, scars
of substance, abuse of the
flesh by the brain,
what damage, what consequences,
what strange becoming of my body
while I sleep?

Episode 11 – March 2015

David Turner: *Why poetry?*

Lizzy Turner: *I think I was intrigued immediately by how language could be used creatively. I think I had that extra perception for it quite early on. Also, you know, you hear a lot of writers and artists talking about how their creative pursuits are more like an affliction than anything else and I think there's definitely that element to it for me as well. I'm quite taken by the stereotype of the tragic romantic artist.*

Hand Torn Edge
Grim Chip

Please do not feed the crack-heads
In the low-brow areas.
It is not advisable
To flaunt your filthy lucre here,
Where your accent is desirable,
Your cover, blown.

As if change was progress.
For richer, for poorer, better or worse,
A caff closes, an estate agent
Opens for business.
As if a manor of thy friends,
Or of thine own.

Episode 13 – March 2015

Grim Chip: *At risk of making a pun at my own expense, I've got a chip on my shoulder about the page/stage stuff. I think there's a danger that if you're known as being good live, people take the attitude, "ok, it can't be all that good written down then." Whereas I actually work really, really hard to make sure it works in both forms, you know, really craft it. I don't think the two things are mutually exclusive.*

Episode 28 – May 2015

Paul McMenemy: *What I think is great about poetry is that it is, at once, immediate and also a kind of slow release. The way things are phrased, the aural effects and so on, can make something hit immediately, but the beauty of poetry is that it will also linger in the mind.*

Guinness Ross, 16 years and 2 miles on
Paul McMenemy

On the Trongate, in the rain, he had cut
his hair and put on weight. In my unironic
suit with Poundland bag I greet the unchanged chronic
grin on this medieval hamsterman and shut
the sadcase greet that fills me like a waterbutt;
I have put on weight and cut my hair. Chthonic
and unmanned, remote the lighter fuel and tonic
days, we look each other in the shoes and tut,

> "Fuck's sake, it's not like we're dead!
> We've both got work, for once,
> and nothing to do with the night
> but drink five pints and head.
> Nostalgia, you beaming dunce,
> drink up, then get out of my sight."

Waking of Insects
Donald Chegwin

The windowsill is a mausoleum for dead insects.
Ants, flies, wasps, spiders, a lone beetle
all entombed in thick grey dust-blankets.
Until you return home, honey, I refuse to hoover up dead insects
because only a dead insect truly understands how I feel.

Until you return home, honey, I shall dine on nothing but tinned
      curries.
I'll always make two portions – one for you, one for me –
and I'll keep on eating your portion until the day you return home.

Honey, I imagine one of the first things you'll point out when you walk
      through the door is that the kitchen floor is flooded.
I think a valve in the tap has probably snapped.
You might notice one of my old socks is lying stranded in the water.
How I empathise with that sock: lost, lonely, separated from its partner.
Socks come in pairs, honey!
Socks come in pairs!

Breakfast: one tinned curry for me, one tinned curry for you.

The bookshelf has collapsed
and charity shop books lie mangled together on the carpet
like ingredients in a strange and unsuccessful recipe.
The toilet won't flush.
The front door won't shut properly.
Burglars might burgle me, murderers might murder me.
Let them come.

Ants roam in the honey jars.
Let them roam.
Let them roam I say
until the day you return home
and then I'll set the hoover on 'em and suck 'em up and laugh as they
     perish
or I'll scoop 'em up and take 'em out outside without harming a single
     one of 'em
(you choose honey you choose).

Lunch: One tinned curry for me, one tinned curry for you.

You're still my princess and there's your throne.
No one will be allowed to sit in your throne until you return home,
     honey.
Not even my parents.
Not even my grandmother.
I'd rather make my grandmother sit on the floor
than let her sit on your throne, honey,
even though she's 84 and has bad knees.

Dinner: one tinned curry for me, one tinned curry for you.

Work used to keep phoning me.
Left me messages asking where I was.
They don't phone anymore.
They sent through my P45.

Breakfast: one tinned curry for you, one tinned curry for me.

Until you return home, honey, I'll walk on all fours and I'll scream like
     a fox in mating season until the neighbours pound on my door
     and shout that they're going to call the police
but they're fucking lying, they won't call the police, they're cowards.

Until you return home, honey,
I'll keep drinking every night.
I'll keep on waking up in graveyards
and on doorsteps
and in strange unclean beds
with no memory of how I got there
and paranoia snacking on my senses.

Until you return home honey,
I won't change my clothes.
I won't mend my ways.
I won't separate night from day.
I'll speak in tongues.
I'll refuse to clean.
I'll listen to nothing but white noise.
I'll watch nothing but static.
I'll talk to the cockroaches and the rats
about the old Steve Martin movies we used to watch together.

I've been eating tinned curries for five years.
I'm expecting you back any day now, honey.

Episode 31 – May 2015

Donald Chegwin: *With my writing there's probably a blur between flash fiction, short stories and poetry, but also with performance poetry; there's so much you can do with it, so many influences, from hip hop to comedy to folk music. I love the fact that there are no 'rules' in comparison to what I learned at school about poetry [...] I've got several poems that are just recipes!*

Episode 51 – January 2016

Lizzy Turner: *Perhaps you could talk a little about your interactive poems?*

Abi Palmer: *Something that really interests me about writing is the idea of using metaphors. The conflict that arises when you have metaphor that makes you approach something from a different angle or a space that you hadn't considered previously. I'm really into these connections and juxtapositions and I wondered how far these things could go beyond 'just' words, so I started to write poems in which the reader is totally immersed.*

Drinking Game (mine's a *Dark and Stormy*)
Abi Palmer

because the windows fail to shut their eyes to darkness / mould will swarm my ancient loaf of bread / disease and little girls go nameless / wrongly named and renamed yet again / Change has a new look / unfortunate heels and a satin dress / but you will know her from her plucked brows / her purple veins / nothing settles / sell your flat / buy a new car / cram the contents of your bookshelves into someone else's houseboat / don't forget to close the blinds & raise another dozen

to every year lost to sleep / to nothing dreams / to bedrest / to a chaise longue / a padded couch / a stinking blanket / reruns of F.R.I.E.N.D.S and friendless / films watched alone and not remembered / to drowsy fog of breakfast porridge / raisins brought on trays at 10am / to morning mantras: "How are you?" / "How was the traffic?" / days of only watching others fold the laundry / slowly out-of-place CDs / books on the wrong shelf / sheets of paper shuffled with no sense of prayer / to *can you cope with that?* / *will you be okay?* / pause for lunch / pause for dinner / end of day forgotten teeth / a dirty set of old pyjamas / late night scrolling / crescent eyes / malaise / repeat / repeat / repeat / to fade

Introduction – Part Two

David Turner: [...] Going back to the start, back at the Dragon Café, when I saw someone read a poem. It was one of the few times in my life where it really felt like a lightbulb had gone off in my head.

I realised that what I wanted to do was talk to people. Perhaps there was something in this medium that would allow me a way of articulating a truth about what I was feeling. I wanted to communicate in a way that wasn't centring myself and was accessible for other people. Also, having spent five weeks on John Dickson, a secure psychotic specialist ward, it taught me very plainly that not everyone who goes through those things has the ability to talk about their experiences afterwards.

I came out of that experience feeling as though I had an obligation, because if I ever felt I could talk about my mental illness, then I probably should. I suppose the last four and a half years since coming out of the hospital, what I've been trying to learn along the way, is what was an appropriate time to share those feelings in conversations? What is the right way of talking about your own experiences that would allow space for other people to talk about themselves?

I haven't found the answer and I am probably unlikely ever to find that answer, because of course it varies from person to person, experience to experience and moment to moment. Again, it goes back to your motivations. If you're seeking that, people will probably sense it and trust you more.

Abi Palmer: Something that's always fascinated me about the podcast series is the diversity of poetic voices and styles on

offer. Would you say that starting a dialogue about poetry was more interesting to you than the poetry itself?

Well it's interesting. When Lizzy and I first started interviewing people, early on, the first question would always be *why poetry?*

I've sort of stopped asking that, or I do ask it, but in more nuanced ways and I try to tailor it to each guest, but it was really important for me to find out *why* would you be doing this? Why are you here, sharing these ideas, to what aim, to what end?

I think this project, this series, has given me a way to keep shouting into the void that is the internet: *Why poetry?* It really could be: *Why anything?* It's the *why* that's the important bit. I don't understand why people listen, why people come on as guests, I don't understand why I'm doing this, but it doesn't matter, because it's happened and I can't say it isn't happening, because it's there, isn't it?

The Why? question is almost every poem ever written, isn't it? What you've got is a series of Whys? framed in different language. When people are reading their poems and you're having different Why? conversations with each guest, that's what a poem is. Different ways of having the same conversation and using language to explore this big, existential hole we're in. An interesting thing about poetry is it's something that's held up by both the left and the right wing in different ways as this high art, but also this complete waste of time.

This has been the most productive waste of time in my life. I think we're really lucky as humans in the West that we are afforded a space to waste our time and it should be embraced.

It's difficult, sometimes, if you say to a poet: *It's really great you've got a way of wasting your time.* People take it personally, as if you're saying there's no point.

But that's the thing with how art is viewed in the West (because it's a very Westernised view). It's what you do in your spare time. This is why class politics is so important to me, because not everyone is afforded the time to play around.

Not everyone is afforded the ability or permission to waste time, whether that's because they're from a background where it's heavily frowned upon and they're judged for what they're doing, they physically can't engage with something, or they are not allowed to identify their own gender or sexuality in public.

I was just thinking about the luxury of self-expression linking to the luxury of self. The luxury of being allowed to be exactly who you are, or explore the parts of you that you don't understand yet. We need language for that. The fact that there are new recognised words: *non-binary* as a gender identity, or *gaslighting* as a type of trauma: if we didn't play with language and create space for questions, we wouldn't have created the language to identify what's actually going on in our lives.

Politically, if you see campaigns about other governments and other regimes, to varying and horrifying degrees of punishment, very often what we're protesting is denial of freedom of expression and it's really poisonous for people to be denied a way to self-identify.

Fabulous

Travis Alabanza

Click fingers.
Fall to the floor.
Yaaass hunty,
click clack,
cunt-y-did-you-not-see-her-fall?

Death Drop. To Drop Dead.
They hear me when I scream, fabulous.
Did they not hear you scream, fabulous?
Did you die on beat, how fabulous.
Oh you know violence? She's fabulous, you'll have to meet.

Cross your fingers, click them,
Z formation and hope to die.
Quick and painless, 3 minutes 32 seconds.
Instead of this long drawn out walk.
One heel in front of the other.

It snaps.
You snap.
Break back.
Clap.
Now lets do it all again next weekend.

Episode 57 – February 2016

Travis Alabanza: *I wish I could tell my younger self, don't listen to what they say is 'poetry'. Find what you think is great, read it, love it, and then just keep on practising. I feel like black writers have this extra inner voice in them, telling them not only that what they're writing isn't good, but that they can't even write - I still sometimes question if I can write. I think I would just say, find other writers that speak like you, start looking at poetry in a broader sense of words, and then start realising that the music artists you see creating shit, these are rhymes that you can then take and create into poetry. [I would] just tell my younger self to keep on doing it!*

Episode 61 – February 2016

David Turner: *Something I've thought about a lot is why people ask, "what are you trying to say with your work?" and not, "what are you trying to ask with your work?"*

Keith Jarrett: *Exactly! I'm full of loads of opinions but I'm not exactly full of answers! The more I respond to what's going on around me, the more questions I find.*

Granddad's Conspiracy of Yams
Keith Jarrett

At night, because it is southern Florida,
and because of that summer with the spray-killed
orange trees in every neighbourhood, the government
men arrive in sleeveless jumpsuits and clipped tongues.

As one, they hurdle the fence, measure out the space
between the blades of grass, detect the mounds
of earth you handled; each one they replace with stones.
Hard, small. Not at all the size of what's unearthed.

In silence they work: spades, rakes, gloves, gun, spray.
A snake hiss. The mist of poison set to work on ground
you've cultivated since you first arrived in southern Florida.
They zip it up in body-sized bags. Their badges catch the light.

They alone know the power of your hands. In southern
Florida, at night, they disrupt the earth in your garden
the earth you've so carefully tended
the earth which now tends to you.

Etiquette Quartet
Anna Kahn

i
The model onscreen has so many
labial piercings that the man
whose turn it is
is unsure how to proceed.

The model reaches down
makes room for him among the rings,
practiced at navigating herself
triangulated with the viewer.

I like to imagine management
in the actual-backest-room
back rooms of sex clubs
bickering over what porn to play.

ii
You can insert a very slight
brittleness into your voice
to tell a practiced swinger
that his conversation

isn't going to segue into anything else.
This tone is almost undetectable.
The deal is that he will keep
talking to you for another few minutes

(face-saver, pretence that he really is
interested in talking to you about gardens)
then the magic words: *well,*
I'll leave you to it, and he'll wander off.

iii
Swingers love to tell you
their jobs. Kinksters keep this secret
so I generally deflect: *oh, this time I'll be*
an international...erm...bookseller.

A man who is not even the man
I am politely brittle-voicing,
a man I am literally
never going to have sex with

pipes up from the sidelines:
you are writing a book, yes?
For a moment I think he knows
something. It's fine. He misheard.

iv
Eventually they all bloody
wander off and I can say
to the man I actually came
to sit next to (full sleeve tattoo,

thick arms, Dutch name too
distinctive for this poem,
very patient in the face
of these distractions):

no pressure but would you
like to have sex with me?
He says, *what pressure?*
Let's do this.

Episode 65 – March 2016

Anna Kahn: *I'm a bit of an electricity junkie I suppose [...] if you go to somewhere like 'Forget What You Heard' or 'Boomerang Club' or many other events, you are guaranteed long periods of electricity where you're hanging on the edge of your seat. I think as a performer it's really easy to generate that electricity in these spaces because the audiences are really up for that [...] It's like poetry as an act of huge intensity, as violence.*

Until The Last Light Goes Out I Was Still Here
Melissa Lee-Houghton

Don't talk to me about discipline – I just stood outside
smoking with no pants on and I'm not even pissed. Out of
sleepers, my insomnia is so rampant I've taken every soporific
drug left in the house just to engorge the next four hours so it
fills the hole. You want to look at me. You want to look at me.
You look at me – I'm the last person you want to look at. Trust
me, it doesn't matter how far down you descend, when they
say 'spiral' they mean 'sheer drop', and yes, when there's no-
where left to go you'll find a recess, you'll find a back alley, or
a bad dream, or a waiting room, or a black out; it's there; you
won't have to struggle far to reach it. There is no end. It goes
on forever; I dream of a house and every room is empty. I look
for you – in a thousand and sixty-nine nights I have not once
sensed you there. Sometimes there is a broken chair, a falling
curtain, but no body, no bloodstream. I get wet thinking about
the needle you're holding.

      You make a scale model of my life. There's the park
bench, and the graveyard; the people looking on; the jumpers;
you haven't made me yet; you're worried I'll look different,
there's more I can lose; the pain is unquantifiable – it doesn't
quite work as a 3D art-piece, for all your efforts – you can't
fashion clay into a realistic ghost. You can't bear to touch
the parts of me you'd have to fix.

                    When you go, turn out the
light for the last time. I'll have to feel my way around the walls
to find the switch. And I told her when the switch goes on
I can write it – but you know there is no switch. I say a lot of
things for money and sex; the pain is not palatable, I know;

maybe if we re-model the book as a script and draft in Michael Fassbender. Someone attractive in place of me; minus the scars – the scars could sell, but then again, your readers think they want to see them, but they crave the smooth skin those other writers wear for bed. So turn out the light; if I'm crying, just pretend you have somewhere to be; yeah I know you're lying. Yeah I always know you are. Don't worry about it – who would want to lie next to me? No one sleeps next to the ravine, do they? Or do they? Oh, the junkies, yeah. Oh, and the molested. Oh, and the emotionally replete; and no, these hundred beds I've died in this year didn't like me either; I left them so clean; it was almost as if I didn't exist.

Episode 85 – October 2016

Melissa Lee-Houghton: *I think if you always read very different things, you're interested in lots of different art forms, even film and visual art and all sorts, poetry... you can do anything with [it]. I think it's the thing that I'm most into in terms of what I write because it is very dramatic. That, I could turn into a play, I could make it into a sort of dialogue or I could do something [else] with it [...] I like writing that you can change into something else all the time, I don't see it as being very fixed at all. It's never over is it? You can always do something else with it.*

Punky Sue, I Love You
Nadia Drews

Flowered eyes flared, I sat there and stared.
She had sugar-spiked, liquorice stick hair.
With ripple-dripped lips, blackcurrant lolly licked hips,
She shone sherbert white through mohair.

On the smacked lino floor by the battered back door
I sat down no protest and saw
With horror bag crisps, as she spoke smoke-wisped lisps
Of wounds she had got in her war.

Glue-stuck to her side sniffed limp lifeless cries
From a sickly gripped jelly baby boy.
Cough-dropped dummied tot from a bleak sheetless cot
No peek-a-boo, toy hiding joy.

She told the big girls what she knew of the world,
Of benefits, costs, lost fist fights,
Of what you should give, how often and how
Tattooed tracks marked lifelines black as night

She watched the cracked clock and when she took the knock,
We were kicked out. She cursed and she swore,
She'd never been glad to see those bad lads,
But they kept on knocking for more.

Well, she did a flit when she'd got sick of it,
And it turned out 'she wasn't so fit',
And riddled, slag lads bragged what they had had,
And popping space dust turned to grit.

But I'd been there, I'd seen what a loveheart she'd been,
A bubblegum sticker for keeps,
And when I'm on the floor and I've locked the back door,
I savour the taste of cheap sweets.

Episode 86 – October 2016

Nadia Drews: *Music and politics are the things that have shaped anything that I've put on paper. I was brought up by my mother who has had a lifelong commitment to socialism [...] In middle age, what I'm still trying to act on are those impulses from my teenage years. I think the world is rotten to its core and I believe that music and other art forms, like poetry, can play a role in lifting people's spirit to change it.*

The Gate
Nick Makoha

The last I remember there were three of us
running, travelling through ochre dust following
fireflies as long as the path decided.

If we had stayed in our village we would have become
lives carved open. Would you believe I used to play
hide-and-seek in these woods, by the high grass,

using the night rains as cover? The road's shoulder
was a marker. Lorries would bully their way over
the tarmac. Their headlamps were corridors of light

that you could use to pick up speed. The earth
would take your weight if you danced along it.
There is a way of leaning into an evening's camber

with all your momentum that turns you and the world
into one. If you ask, the river will hold your breath
in a covenant of silence. My brother used to wonder

how I disappeared after his ten count. With one palm
in front of the other, like a drunk sleepwalker,
he would push himself into the night to look for me.

Episode 88 – November 2016

David Turner: *Having benefitted from access to writing collectives do you feel an obligation to help others?*

Nick Makoha: *Not an obligation, [however,] I want to be a good writer, and I want to be a good writer among other great writers. I don't want to leave a situation worse than the one I found, so I hope when my time is done as a writer, there will be avenues for other writers that weren't necessarily there for me when I was starting out. I think it's vital because there's no direct pathway to being a poet or writer of any description.*

Episode 89 – December 2016

Harry Josephine Giles: *I think, at heart, access is about learning how to treat everyone around you as a human who deserves connection, and that there are loads of different types of humans, and your assumption about what a human might need is usually wrong - you have to actually listen to what they need and then try and help.*

Why I am not in the Book
Harry Josephine Giles

I am not in the Book
as the Book did not ask.

No I am not in the Book
becos the Boke asked
& I sed No.

No I sayed Yes
becos the Buke aksed
& then I was not
in the Buik becos I sed
N   o   .

Yes I sed Yes
& then I sayed No.

I sed No 2 the Book
the Boke the Buik
2 which I sayed Yes
becos 2 B Me
in the Book was 2 B
the only Me that could B
in the Beuk that was in
the Book & the Boke
did not ask Me
the Boke only aksed
Me & so I sed No
2 the Buke I sed Yes 2.

2 which I said Yes.

The Book 2 which
I sayed Yes 2 which
I sayed No 2 which
did not aks Me
planted a seed in my gut
which grew 2 a stalk
at the hed of the stalk
was a giant who pulped
my brayn B 4
I said Yes which is why
I said No 2 the Book
2 which I said No
2 2 2 which I said Yes.

2 whit: I said No
2 the Boak th Boak th Boak
2 which did not ask
Me as it aksed
Me & then
I sed Yes & then
I sayed No No No No No No
2 the Boak 2 which
I sed 2 who 2 whit —

Did U No? that the Owl
which we hear as 2whit-

2who is not 1 Owl
but 2 2-whit
& 2-who which I learned
from the Buke as I learned
from my seeded heart
there is somewhere 1 Owl
who says: 2wit2woo.

I am not in the Book
becos Boak Boak Boak.

No I am not
in the Buke becos
I said No to the Buke
that was Boak was Boak
was a Book 2 which I said
N o .

I am not in the Beuk
as I didno No if the Book
ever knew I was Real
was a Yes a Yes a Yes
on the Skin of the Buik
that says Yes.

The Book that sed No
2 the Yes that was Me
was the Boak 2 which
I sayed No 2 the Boak
that sed No that aksed
that did not No that aksed
2 which I sayed Yes
which then sed Yes
2 who 2 who 2 who?

2 whom did the Book
2 which I sayed No
say yes?
2 whom 2 whom 2 whom?

Whom sed
Yes 2 the Buik
2 which I said No?

Whom said Yes 2 the Me
that was Skin Skin Skin
in the Boke that Sayed Yes
2 the I that sayed Me
in the Skin of the Book?

I sayed Yes 2 the Me
that was Yes in the Skin
of the Book & so
I sed No to the Book
2 which I sed Yes.

2 the Buke 2 which
I sed Yes I say Booooak.

I say Yes to the Book to the
Boak to the Buke to the Buik
to the Book the Book the
Book the B the B the Book
the Ook the Ook Ook the
Ook Book OK the Book the
OK Ook Book the OK the
Book OK the OK the O O O O

Introduction – Part Three

Abi Palmer: When we first met, you actually told me *I f**king hate poetry*. Do you still feel like that?

David Turner: Part of me is a bit embarrassed that I used to so proudly go round saying how much I hated poetry. But it was true. It's still true, but for slightly different reasons now, the deeper I'm in it. I hate poetry in the same way I hate fine art and I love fine art. If people ask me what I mean, I don't understand how they can't see how close love and hate are interlinked.

What I think has changed now about what I hate about poetry is slightly different, because if you view what I said early on as a rejection of the established idea of what poetry is, I have to accept that now, four years into running a poetry podcast, I am establishment. Not that I'm an established voice or opinion, but I'm as established as anything I would have rejected at the start.

What I hate now about poetry is still about refusing access to certain people. I find most people I meet intensely interesting, and I think everyone, as much as possible, deserves to have their say about this thing they love. This is what I mean about not being establishment. I am a gatekeeper, because I run a series and I choose who comes on. But I want to be as generous a gatekeeper as possible.

Has your role as a more established gatekeeper changed your perspective on what it means to provide access to the podcast and its conversations?

I've realised that what it means to make something accessible

48

is not what I envisaged at the beginning. In the same way as what I was rejecting in the term 'poetry', or the idea of poetry, the idea of what access is, is far broader than I imagined at the beginning. Most of what you're talking about when you're talking about access are not things I experience myself.

I'm able-bodied, I still have pretty good hearing, I'm white and cisgendered. I probably at one point felt that if I just made something, just transcribed an episode, that would make it accessible, and of course, it goes a long way, but it isn't what access is. I've learnt along the way how insulting it is to claim you're making something accessible when it's not to someone, how disheartening and upsetting, and one of many repeated blows that person receives in their life.

Do you think it's your responsibility to challenge that? How have you challenged that as a podcaster?

If anyone asks my advice on how to run a successful interview-based podcast, you just really have to listen to your guest. If you're going to have conversations around difficult subjects.... These are not difficult subjects per se, these are very emotive to people and when they're done wrongly, they are very painful to the people they affect.

For example, if you're trying to talk about access for the hard-of-hearing to an audio production such as a podcast, you cannot have that conversation unless it primarily involves someone that is hard of hearing. You need to offer full editorial control, and to give them the platform. Not just the chance for a soundbite, or to give you enough opinion that you can then chop up and frame for your own editorial viewpoint... Give over the microphone and let them talk about how it's affected them. And then acknowledge that this is a single person's experience of the world and that every other hard-of-hearing person engaging with that conversation will probably not have experienced it in quite the same way.

Is there anything you can do as a podcaster to support the people you're offering a platform to?

As much as possible, I try and extend conversations onto social-media platforms. It doesn't always work, but I think that's been my main mode of thinking. If I was aware of a conversation through social media or through friends, or attending events, I would try to find someone whose artistic practice already encompassed talking about these things to facilitate the conversations. That's why Harry Giles was invited to host our 'Access to the Arts' conversation. That's why Khairani Barokka was invited for 'Access to Publishing'. That was why Paula Varjack was invited to talk about artists being paid. All three of these people had already made it their point to publicly talk about these subjects.

That means you've got somebody who's informed about the subject. It also means you're not burdening a person to come up with a whole episode for you from scratch. If I'm giving editorial control to someone, my job then is to identify what is most important to that person and try and maintain those elements, whilst trying to juggle the budget, if there is a budget, juggle the logistical side of things, and be there as a producer. There are different roles in a podcast: you're host, editor and producer, sometimes all at once.

How do you juggle that?

It's really hard. It happens more naturally now, but I don't think it's necessarily any easier, it just suddenly becomes habit. It's still exactly the same amount of energy. The nature of a single host/editor/producer-based podcast is that you have to be present in the conversation, aware of background noise, make sure your guest is comfortable, the recorder is on, still on, still on, listen to your guest, do not stop listening to your guest...

Can I also say, I've learnt how to shut the f**k up?

Did getting Arts Council funding change your experience of being a podcaster?

I can't say anything other than it revolutionised everything I did. It made all the ideas I had possible overnight. It was amazing. The Arts Council has its flaws and the application process is littered with issues, but there is no way I could deny the positive effects having money suddenly had on the project, It meant I could go and talk to the people I wanted to. I could travel to Belfast or Torquay, travel to Leeds and dedicate a whole episode to poets who also worked as playwrights, resulting in the episode 'Poetry & theatre-making in West Yorkshire.' I could only have dreamed about focusing on such a niche subject, which turned out to be a really rich couple of conversations.

That's probably where the motivation to apply for money came from. It was becoming something I really didn't want it to be, which was a London-based podcast, because I could only afford to get to people if I could use my Oyster card. I couldn't just keep waiting for people to come to me.

Up-Lit
Luke Kennard

It is best to start with something small. Pick a leaf from a tree. Tear it. Hold it to your face. Taste it. What are you directly experiencing? For this moment, all you are thinking about is the leaf. Maybe you don't want to pick a leaf. I am going to suggest that you do it anyway. In the West we believe you have a theory and you put it into practice. This is a misconception. You have a *praxis* and by that praxis you one day hope to attain *thereia*.

In time you will find this comes as naturally to you as your heart beat, as inhaling and exhaling, as reaching for your next cigarette.

There will never be another moment like this one and there has never been a moment like this one in the whole of human history. If you do not like the moment you may say to yourself, *The vibration of energy known as myself is vibrating in a way which does not give the vibration of energy known as myself pleasure.* But what is pleasure to a vibration of energy? Did the leaf you picked feel pain when you tore it? I very much hope not.

Arrange your desk lamp so that it floods the wall to your left with light. Hold up your hand so that it makes a shadow puppet of a happy looking ram with a fat nose. Move your little finger to make him say, 'Great!'

One of your sons from your first marriage has been serially cyber-bullying his fellow students   via social networks. He has been doing this for two years and it has only emerged because one of his victims has tried to take her own life.

His behaviour may not even be connected to your affair and subsequent divorce and there is little to be gained from blaming yourself for it. Of course the vibration of energy known as your ex-wife wants you to talk to him. He has not expressed the slightest remorse and seems incapable of doing so.

There is nutmeg on your cappuccino. Did you even ask for nutmeg? It seems foolish of the barista to assume such an unusual taste would be appetising to just anyone, so maybe he got your order mixed up with someone else's.

What you might tell the vibration of energy known as your son is that he also should live in the moment. The tips of your fingers are pressing plastic, spring-loaded "keys" to deposit "language" in a series of boxes which are really only projections of light. Perhaps it will help him to live in the moment if he injures his fingertips slightly – or even severely – so that every key-stroke causes discomfort.

But for now there is the baby, and your new wife and the sense that even your best actions now form part of an enormous betrayal. *The vibration of energy known as myself believes himself to be party to an enormous betrayal.* Resist metaphor. The vibration of energy known as yourself should not be likened to the vibration of the muzzle of a discharging automatic weapon. The vibration of energy known as yourself should not be compared to a rabbit shuddering with myxomatosis. The vibration of energy known as yourself should reach up to a low-hanging branch and pluck another leaf.

Episode 94 – March 2017

Luke Kennard: *I remember it as a slightly bleak time where I nearly gave up writing completely. I had written two novels which had completely failed. There isn't even anything good to fillet from them for a short story really. They were just long, long failures. [I] didn't have any idea for what to try to do for my next novel or poetry book [...] it was like, "oh my god, absolutely nobody cares!"*

[...]

David Turner: *You were close to completely knocking the writing on the head?*

LK: *Yeah, that's how I felt at the time. I'd go on long walks in the evening to sulk.*

DT: *Was this out of the ordinary for you? Was it a shock?*

LK: *A little yeah, because it's the only thing I'm good at. In a way it was a bit of a temper tantrum as much as anything else.*

DT: *I have that about every three months where I want to jack everything in!*

Naeema
Amerah Saleh

I sit on the right-hand corner of your inflatable bed.
The air is slowly being released without me realising.

I hold your hand in a crowded room of faces I've spent years
     erasing,
like rubbing out pen marks with a blue rubber.
Your hands used to have the potential to be Nivea-model-like.
Now they're dry,
like you've given up on the chance for people to love you.

I lean to your cold but regal face and call out *Nan*.
It's me.
Amerah.

Your breaths
inside my head
say you know.
I am stood in a room,
hood up.
I am 8 again and you are teaching me to hold my balance on
     6 wheel rollerblades.
I am 7 again and you're sneaking us into your room to give us
     mint or orange club bars without our parents finding out.
I am 6 again and you are standing outside our school gates with
     sweets.
I am 5 again and we are feeding the ducks every Saturday in
     Cannon Hill Park.
I am 24 and sat beside you with my lips to your forehead trying
     to say goodbye.

Episode 94 – March 2017

Amerah Saleh: *We're very lucky to be in a world where young people are getting, not just seats at the table, but full on hours at the table to have those conversations about our history. About what it means to be black or Muslim at this time. We [Beatfreeks] are so lucky to be able to provide those platforms and spaces for young people to do that.*

Episode 95 – March 2017

Khairani Barokka: *So, 'Indigenous Species' is not a poetry collection, it is one poem and the introduction is basically an essay that introduces that poem. [...] I consider myself an interdisciplinary artist. I was trained in interdisciplinary mixed media art, which is weirdly how I rediscovered poetry because I always wrote poetry since I was a toddler.*

epitaph
Khairani Barokka

the great barrier reef comes knelling to the reaper,
and now antarctica. everything's a-crumble.

come hither, says the angel at the gates,
revealing not-lustlessness. more on this later.

a friend who only wanted to make the doctors feel
much better around her was buried today, and her spouse

will remember. "we'll be gone if the end days are soon,
as we're in our thirties," someone says to me post-funeral.

thinking about the end is not the point of flowing arteries;
feeling about it strains us—the waste poured into candy crush

must come from some horrible bosses' spiking of anxiety in us,
partially. a reaching out for a friend who leaves must

turn some slights to bludgeons. and last year, i witnessed
a family saying it was fine for a baby to hit other children.

whole languages dying while i hypocritically write in one
i refuse to speak with my mother. *come, come hither,*

says the angel at the gates, *i am of a sex that does
not yet exist in the world of* homo sapiens. *i made god*

*give me some strange light between these legs,
so when you arrive, you will know: there is still the new.*

Ransom Tape
Joe Dunthorne

A boom or some fruit keeps bobbing into frame.
Our children are dressed in tracksuits the colour of aubergines.
They kneel in a clearing of sawgrass somewhere between
the equator and the Tropic of Capricorn. It feels wrong to say
the production values reassure us. At the press conference,
we make it clear we will not pay.

                                                            We pay,
handing a holdall to young men in Wendy's, Caracas,
while our kids, wrists tied, wait politely
in the accessible restroom; it opens from both sides.

Episode 96 – April 2017

Joe Dunthorne: *I just thought of [how] people [think that] most writers are either planners or non-planners. I'm a non-planner, and I think what I enjoy, and keep going back to, is not knowing, and sitting down and being surprised. That seems addictive and has seemed addictive ever since I first tried it, this idea of not having something and then two hours later having something you couldn't have guessed.*

Episode 101 – June 2017

Zeina Hashem Beck: *What I would like for [my poetry night] 'Punch' to do is to maybe inspire someone sitting in the audience to start their own night, whether it be something curated, or open mic, or whether it's just a workshop where we're saying, "let's talk about poetry," just to tell the younger people, "you can start something." Don't be scared, just start it and see what happens.*

Apparition
Zeina Hashem Beck

The woman on your balcony
looks familiar. You offer her coffee
& she sips, reminds you to get
that lightbulb in the kitchen fixed, let go
of that old eyeshadow
(it's been years) talk to your mother
more often. You tell her you dreamt
your daughter was sleeping
like the children on the news,
& she asks if she can borrow
your black leather jacket—
she loves the studs & silver zippers,
she's tired of roving in this gown
like this world's merely a visit
she has to make on morning rounds
to the ill. You tell her
your husband doesn't like to read
the credits at the end of movies,
always leaves you alone in your seat
& this scares you. She goes inside
& down the stairs. She hums, the way
you sometimes do in supermarket aisles,
the tremors in your throat
taking you by surprise
between the grapes & the strawberries,
& you almost whispering
Hello.

My Sister and the Wolves
Kim Moore

It's been a year since my sister began
to live with wolves. Each night the sound
of their slow breathing fills her house
and in the morning they sing her awake.

All the wolves who live outside belong to her
and all the ones in houses or chained up
in yards and left to howl, all those roaming
the woods, all of these are her children.

She thinks of nothing but wolf. She is all
fields and long coats and hiking boots,
she is all concern at the mice in the shed,
nibbling away at the bags of wolf food,

but it is only wolves that make her heart
ache. She is all clanging gates and kennels
hosed down with water, she spends
her life on the phone to strangers,

negotiating wolf adoptions, convincing
families to take one wolf into their home,
but warning them that with every wolf,
they are also adopting the Moon

and the Night and the Dark, that all
of these things live in the heart
of every wolf she has met. My sister
has room for wolves that are dying,

she has room for wolves that have bitten
small children, she has room for wolves
that don't know their name, she has room
for wolves that are killers of things

like sheep and rabbits and pain.
She takes in wolves that piss
when somebody speaks, wolves
that have never seen a staircase,

wolves that have never walked
on a carpet, wolves whose owners
are bored or stupid or simply vanish.
She takes in wolves of all shapes

and sizes but she will not take in me.
I call to her but no sound I make
will still be made of words by the time
it's crossed the distance between us.

She's moving further and further away.
Last night she was just a cut out on a hill,
the pack at her heels, the sky burning
and I knew she did not belong to me.

Episode 101 – June 2017

Kim Moore: *Teaching in schools has probably been one of the hardest things out of everything I've done [...] but I didn't start writing about it until I went part-time and got a bit of distance from it, I think it's impossible to write about it when you're in it full-time. The connection with teaching and poetry is, as a teacher you get these phrases that you come out with all the time, like catchphrases, and sometimes they are like lines of poetry, and you use language to, hopefully, make the children laugh.*

Episode 103 – July 2017

Rishi Dastidar: *[My] book 'Ticker-tape' is a classic example of how editorial care, support, attention, intervention makes something five, ten, twenty times better. Every writer needs an editor [...] there is no writer that cannot be made better with some form of intervention.*

Prophet Kean in The End Times
Rishi Dastidar

She is reading a book about
    death,

not yours or mine but everybody
    else's,

and yet this does not trouble her
    unduly

as she knows that for you, me,
    everybody,

the end is actually the best
    beginning,

the thing to which we are truly
    addicted –

starts afresh, new pages, green lights,
    go signs.

In another dream, I fete her as a
    prophet

not because she gives me a date to
    check out

but instead the first dance after
    eternity.

Introduction – Part Four

Abi Palmer: I like the podcast as an object for poetry because you can pause it, and share it, and listen when you're ready. Has the podcast format shaped your experience of the poetry and the conversations you've been having?

David Turner: One of the reasons I'm embarrassed about listening to older episodes I'm in is because my opinions and knowledge have changed so much. But you have to embrace that, I think. That's part of being an artist. Or it's part of how a lot of people are artists. Some people will maintain a very firm identity, a narrow set of rules for the way they create art. Most of us are just bouncing through the universe from one idea to the next and it's natural things will change.

The podcast format has been a way to form a dialogue. My main editorial thought when I'm in a conversation with someone is that I'm not actually in conversation with my guests alone, I'm in conversation with the audience. As the audiences have steadily grown over the last four years, so has my awareness of an obligation. If you're demanding an hour or an hour and a half of someone's attention, you need to bear them in mind.

What have you learnt about your audience?

That they're really loyal and exceptionally broad-minded, because they seem to equally stick with any guest I put in front of them. It's amazing to think hundreds of people tune in. Most of my audience must not know most of my guests because I don't necessarily know people before I get to talk to them.

I went to Istanbul in March 2015 and interviewed eight writers I met over the course of three days. I knew nothing of their work. People continue to download these back episodes and listen to them.

Often I will see that people have returned three or four times to a particular episode. It's really nice. That's the exact difference and why I love podcasts over radio, because there's a pressure to be present for the radio. A podcast serves the same purpose as a journal in that you can lay it down on the table and come back to it when you're ready.

Another thing I've learnt about my audience is that it's global. Apart from the two polar continents, there are listeners on every continent. It's really beautiful to be able to give a poet the opportunity to communicate with those people.

It's also worth acknowledging that Lunar Poetry Podcasts are being archived in the British Library. They're now a body of literature that's been collected. What did that mean to you?

I was hugely proud of that. It sort of runs up against my personality, but I really felt I'd achieved something, because it meant these disparate voices were suddenly in a really established archive. It meant that someone like Mishi Morath, who I've become friends with, and is someone that doesn't even class themselves as a poet and in his own words is *just an open-micer* is now in a national archive, which will be forever preserved... until we're taken over by the ants.

And so we've come to the point where we've got a podcast about poetry that is now going to be made into an anthology of poetry. We've come full circle. What made you want to put a book together in this form?

Right from the beginning, I didn't shy away from the fact I wanted to keep the word 'poetry' in the title, so it became Lunar Poetry Podcasts. When I started, the fashion was to talk only of spoken word and to frame it as a spoken-word project, but I wanted to root it firmly in the act of writing poetry and the tradition of printing poetry on paper. The oral tradition in poetry and storytelling is much longer but it was only the advent of the printing press that made any form of literature accessible, because it meant you didn't have to be sitting in the presence of the person telling the story.

I didn't want to lose touch with that. It seemed natural to go from the written word to the spoken word to the recorded voice to a digital form, to then return back to a paper form.

Something that's been interesting about being a guest and also listening to the podcast as a collection is the sheer number of dialogues being churned out one after the other - how they've grown, how they've evolved and the different shapes conversations can take. It's a good reminder that art isn't a fixed object. Whether we're listeners or makers, we're not finished yet.

You've just reminded me of a quote I pulled out by Keith Jarrett and I think it's a beautiful summation. I had said *I've thought about...why people ask, "what are you trying to say with your work?" and not, "what are you trying to ask with your work?"*

His reply was: *I'm full of loads of opinions but I'm not exactly full of answers! The more I respond to what's going on around me, the more questions I find.*

It's so succinct, it almost makes the podcast irrelevant. It just says what everyone has said constantly for 100-odd episodes.

When I Imagine the Sound of It
Sandra Alland

In my dream
Philip DeWilde reactivates Facebook
and posts on his memorial wall:
'I hate this vvvv'

above strangers talking about themselves;
people he was no longer talking to;
misogynist screen grabs I'd give my skin to unread

Philip DeWilde links to a video:
him flying over a Florida beach;
his youngest brother hangs from one foot

It's a dream so he doesn't need a cape or wings,
though he does have a purple balloon;
it casts a shadow over Adam's smile
as he clutches Philip DeWilde's left flip-flop

The waves crash like cars: often;
surprising us with their power
though we really should know by now

Philip DeWilde shouts:
Don't worry, I didn't go to the funeral or memorial either.
Even your death isn't your own!
Though I liked Mike's YouTube slideshow
and I hear Baba's pastor was fucking hilarious.

And Philip DeWilde's shadow
becomes a string of emojis:
a karate-chopping cat,
a child-dragon rolling around laughing,
then one of those ones that makes you cry harder than it should

Episode 105 – August 2017

Sandra Alland: *I was thinking about what access is. It can be so many things, but can include reducing - and ideally removing - barriers; physical and mental barriers, social barriers, and that includes monetary and governmental barriers; I think we often don't talk about those as much; and linguistic and / or communication barriers to participation, in all facets of life. And then inclusion, for me, leads on from that. I always like to think of it as leaving no one behind. Thinking about and acting upon how to make something possible for as many people as possible - ideally everyone!*

Hard Work and Nudist Beaches
Giles L. Turnbull

As the air I inherited your every sigh.
Urged by the headmaster to take on a stronger role,
I bundled myself with spring beansprouts.
At the village fate everything began to happen,
the young pear engaged in wild passionate scrumpy.

A hoarse runs on loose rain
while lichen turn back into men with the waxing moon.
The usher thinks he's Lord of the Aisles,
dreams of exorcising on the treadmill but,
gammy-legged, still limps to close the gait.

You're so vane, you think the wind blows
in your hair to direct you down the street.
The party is happening in the church haul,
get to your feet and listen to the banned.

Roll up your sleeves, roll down your pants —
so many lives lost over the right to bare arms —
death in the aftermath
of a Friday afternoon
transcription error.

Episode 105 – August 2017

Giles L. Turnbull: *I think the messages about writers from marginalised groups almost certainly is going to start with the people in those groups. I think what needs to be done is that the non-marginalised groups actually listen to those messages and share them so it becomes more widespread. That's one of the biggest things I'm grateful for [with] being blind, it's that I'm much more aware of what's going on in other marginalised communities [...] If somebody wants me to write about blindness I'll do it at the drop of a hat. I give it my priority, because I think it's important the world realises that we all need to be more aware of other people's troubles.*

Episode 108 – November 2017

Susannah Dickey: *It's not the most important thing, to be published, because it's the act of writing and what that gives you [...] It's really lovely to feel like you're getting closer to that stage of producing the kind of material that you really respond to; because, while you like to feel like your work is saying what you want it to, it's also a really nice thought that someone else might be responding to it similarly, in the way that you respond to others' work.*

remove the oboe and the joy would follow
Susannah Dickey

- After 'Leander and Hero' by Hannah Lash

it comes in a fur-lined case like a well-cared for recently
deceased firearm it has its own
screwdriver / smaller than a regular
screwdriver / children are always being given small versions
of regular things and asked to call them toys.
Get ready: you are now the mechanic
of something.
When an oboe gets blown it's a chorus of the throat it's a slow and
ancient courtship it's a clown
car horn. An oboe makes debussy's little
shepherd an asymptote it makes sloop john b a little doughy it makes
its player wet and undignified / low
C or high E flat is three UTIs at once this is because the oboe is a
witch's finger a regular
person's store bought ginger stem. The oboe takes you to the forefront
of an orchestra's mind / it sighs goose loneliness.
The oboe wakes you with the clamminess of its
unplayedness / it puts you in spaces that need to be
filled but does not make you interesting. The oboe is not
enough to recuse you
from your decisions / it isn't a baby or a glass eye / or a relative of
some historical interest. The oboe
[brought out]
[shown off]
is a collective gasp / it is dank breath held separate from the whistling
holes in Wabakimi Provincial Park / the uncontrollable
airs of the rest of the world

A Lover's Manual
Mary Jean Chan

This is the myth of love's tenderness –
that it only heals and cannot wound.
After two decades of spinning around
in space, you hear echoes, wilderness
among stars devoid of human tempers.
Linger there – it is quiet – your breath
audible as the slow burn on a hearth.
Dear lover, how often are you tempted
to infidelity with words, those curious
creatures who only ask that you listen?
Give what love your heart can bear.
Read books that beg only mysterious
thoughts, closed eyes and glistening
palms. Let ink seep into what you hear.

Episode 112 – April 2018

David Turner: *How do you reconcile the aspect of how demanding your work becomes once it's a single-author pamphlet or book? You're not flanked by other writers or sharing a space; now, as a queer writer, you are demanding space in a way that you may not have imagined previously.*

Mary Jean Chan: *It is a very vulnerable experience and I think I was quite surprised at feeling this way, because the aspiration was always working towards a pamphlet and then eventually a full collection. [...] To answer your question, I suppose it just feels like suddenly there is no place to hide. People will be reading the pamphlet and knowing that this is your work and so it's not like you're in 'Poetry Review' and somehow other people's writing is giving yours legitimacy.*

Tilted
Leo Boix

Imagine a day in February, lets say the 24th
   lets suppose it's past 14.00, and you notice

it's the first sunny day in weeks
    that there is a sudden change

in the air

    a tilt,   a shift

a lick warming your face,
   as sun comes out through a clouded sky.

Imagine a room filled with sunlight
   a wooden floor room
with three opened sashed windows
   facing a leafless maple tree,

where a bird feeder hangs
     within a globe

visited by passerine birds

Then your mind travels fast, your room
   is not your room anymore

it's a place you've been long ago,
     but you can't quite recollect.

Imagine *that* room full of birds
          coming to feed

clumsily landing

at your hand.   Then, you remember.

Episode 113 – May 2018

Leo Boix: *I tend to write differently in Spanish and English, I never translate my work from one language to the other. I feel like I'm a different poet, completely, in Spanish and English, the way I write, the imagery, the sensibility in a way. I was born in Argentina, Spanish is my mother tongue. It feels like it's inside me and it comes unfiltered somehow. English is outside me and I can see it physically, I can mould it.*

A British thing to do
Roy McFarlane

standing in queues; queues
appear out of nowhere
and disappear; queues
are filled with weathers
and gossip; queues bulge
ahead with best mates
and family; queues will have
the annoying kid screaming
and twisting; queues
will be colored with tuts
and intakes of frustration
and always *I'm running late*
conversations on mobiles.
Queues held up by the man
with change scattered
across the counter or
the woman with a list
of needs and one last
thought to share.
People wanting tampons
and condoms are rarely
found in queues but you will
find the occasional lovers lost
in each other with signs
of salaciousness still left
over their mouths. Queues
of apologies of *I'll be quick*
and the one behind *what
the hell is holding up this line?*

Queues that begin on Boxing
Day and end on the opening
of New Year Sales; queues
inside and outside buildings,
straight around corners.
And there's always *is this*
what we fought two bloody
world wars to be over-
run by bloody foreigners?

Episode 115 – June 2018

Roy McFarlane: *The number-one thing told to a poet when going*
on a journey of writing poetry: "write what you know." So, no matter
how much I'll read all these incredible poets of the past, half of these
things I don't know. I'll understand the craft, the content maybe, but I
don't 'know' that. But, this [Birmingham and its inhabitants] is what
I know, and I will do everything that I can to translate that into that
form, into that poem.

A Short History of Violence
Jane Yeh

The rush of air.
The fear

Is black and white,
A blur

Just over his head, a feathered
Ball of bad dreams

And someone shouting. A body
Just wants to mind himself,

Keep a blind eye. Out back
A string of lights

Pierces the horizon;
The ground

Races away beneath. He's
Been running for miles

In his ripped jeans, strips
Of T-shirt flapping, dirt

Like a rumor all over him.
His arm a bent lesson

In obedience— not enough.
Out here

Boys are ten a penny,
One less ain't worth

Spilt milk. The pulse
In his throat

Is a bridle against his skin.
The tyre tracks, the smell

Of burning— he can't outrun
The smoke at his back,

Like a panic
Rising. His body

A lamb sheared.

Episode 115 – June 2018

Jane Yeh: *I read a lot of fiction, I always have, ever since I was little.
So, I guess in a way I'm more a fiction writer than a poet because I like
to make up fictional worlds and characters [...] I'm definitely
interested in this idea of thinking of the poem as a collage of lines,
sentences or images and trying to be less linear and less logical in
terms of the construction of the poem.*

THE POETS

Travis Alabanza is an artist based in London who writes, speaks, listens and eats.

Sandra Alland is a writer and interdisciplinary artist living in Glasgow. San has published three poetry collections in Canada, and contributed to over 100 magazines and journals internationally. 2017-18 highlights include: co-editing and touring *Stairs and Whispers: D/deaf and Disabled Poets Write Back* (Nine Arches); publishing stories in three anthologies from Comma Press; and programming the first LGBTQI+ D/deaf and disabled film screening and panel at BFI Flare. San's contribution is from an in-progress long-poem, 'Philip DeWilde Is Dead'. www.blissfultimes.ca

Khairani Barokka's work has been presented in eleven countries, as the recipient of six residencies and multiple grants. Among her honours, she was an NYU Tisch Fellow, and is a UNFPA Indonesian Young Leader. Okka is most recently co-editor of *Stairs and Whispers,* and author of *Indigenous Species* and *Rope.*

Zeina Hashem Beck is an award-winning Lebanese poet. Her second full-length collection, *Louder than Hearts*, won the 2016 May Sarton New Hampshire Poetry Prize. Her work has appeared in *Ploughshares, Poetry, the Academy of American Poets' Poem-a-Day*, and *World Literature Today*, among others. Her poem, 'Maqam', won *Poetry Magazine*'s 2017 Frederick Bock Prize.

Leo Boix is an Argentinean poet based in the UK. He is the author of two collections in Spanish, most recently *Mar de Noche* (Letras del Sur, 2016). His poems have appeared in *PN Review, The Poetry Review, Modern Poetry in Translation (MPT), The Rialto, Litro, Magma Poetry, The Morning Star,* and elsewhere, as well as in many anthologies, such as *Ten: Poets of the New Generation* (Bloodaxe, 2017). Boix is a fellow of The Complete Works scheme.

Mary Jean Chan is a poet and editor from Hong Kong who currently lives in London. She was shortlisted for the 2017 Forward Prize for Best Single Poem, and came Second in the 2017 National Poetry Competition. Mary Jean's pamphlet *A Hurry of English* is published by ignitionpress (2018), and her debut collection is forthcoming from Faber (2019). Mary's poem 'A Lover's Manual' originally appeared in issue 1 of *Anima Magazine*.

Donald Chegwin is a poet and journalist who writes about exquisite meals, Maidstone and unusual creatures. He is currently working on a history of irradiated cuisines. Once he has finished the book, he will burn the manuscript and start again.

Grim Chip is not the man you hoped to meet. Besides which he is a founder member of Poetry on the Picket Line. 'Nuff said.

Rishi Dastidar's debut collection *Ticker-tape* is published by Nine Arches Press, and a poem from it was included in *The Forward Book of Poetry 2018*.

Susannah Dickey's first pamphlet *I had some very slight concerns* was published in 2017 by The Lifeboat. Work has appeared in *The White Review*, *Ambit*, and *Poetry Ireland Review*. Susannah's poem 'remove the oboe and the joy would follow' originally appeared in issue 4 of *The Scores*.

Like the incessant chatter and questioning of her childhood, **Nadia Drews'** songs, plays and poems have needed help with punctuation. She spent a lot of time studying other girls but failed the exam. She took a lot of notes and for some reason some of them rhymed.

Joe Dunthorne's debut novel, *Submarine*, was adapted for film by Richard Ayoade. His second, *Wild Abandon*, won the 2012 Encore Award. His latest is *The Adulterants*. A collection of his poems, *O Positive*, will be published by Faber & Faber next year.

Harry Josephine Giles is from Orkney and lives in Edinburgh. Their latest book is *Tonguit*, shortlisted for 2016's Forward Prize for Best First

Collection, available from Stewed Rhubarb. They are studying for a PhD at Stirling, co-direct the performance producer ANATOMY, and have toured theatre across Europe and Leith. www.harrygiles.org

Melissa Lee-Houghton has published three collections with Penned in the Margins. Her third collection, *Sunshine* won a Somerset Maugham award and was shortlisted for the Costa Book Award, the Ted Hughes Award and the Forward Prizes. She has published a pamphlet with Offord Road Books and a short fiction chapbook with Rough Trade Books.

Former UK poetry slam champion and Rio International Poetry Slam Winner 2014, **Keith Jarrett** is a PhD scholar at Birkbeck University, where he is completing his first novel. His monologue, 'Safest Spot in Town', was aired on BBC Four last summer. His book of poetry, *Selah*, was published in 2017.

Anna Kahn is the host of the Unfinished Edits podcast. She's a Barbican Young Poet and a former member of the Roundhouse Collective. Her work has been published by *The London Magazine, Right Hand Pointing* and The *Rialto*, amongst others. By day she does something inexplicable in tech.

Luke Kennard has published five collections of poetry. He won an Eric Gregory Award in 2005 and was shortlisted for the Forward Prize for Best Collection in 2007. He lectures at the University of Birmingham. In 2014 he was selected by the Poetry Book Society as one of the Next Generation Poets. His most recent collection, *Cain*, was published to great acclaim in 2016 by Penned in the Margins. His debut novel, *The Transition*, was published in 2017 by Fourth Estate. A pamphlet of prose poems, *Truffle Hound*, was published this year by Verve Poetry Press.

Sean Wai Keung's debut pamphlet *you are mistaken* won the inaugural Rialto Open Pamphlet Competition and was named a Poetry School 'book of the year' in 2017. As a writer and performer, he has worked with organisations such as the National Theatre of Scotland, Apples and Snakes and Speculative Books.

Nick Makoha was shortlisted for the 2017 Felix Dennis Prize for Best First Collection for his debut *Kingdom of Gravity*. He is a Cave Canem Graduate Fellow and Complete Works Alumni. He won the 2015 Brunel International African Poetry prize and 2016 Toi Derricotte & Cornelius Eady Chapbook Prize for his pamphlet *Resurrection Man*. 'The Gate' was first published in Nick's debut collection, *Kingdom of Gravity* (Peepal Tree Press).

Roy McFarlane was born in Birmingham of Jamaican parentage and has been Birmingham's Poet Laureate. Roy's contributed to numerous anthologies and enjoyed success with his first collection, *Beginning With Your Last Breath* (Nine Arches Press, 2016). A second collection, *The Healing Next Time*, will be out in October 2018 in which his poem 'A British thing to do' will appear.

Paul McMenemy is six foot tall and don't let anyone tell you otherwise.

Kim Moore's first collection *The Art of Falling* was published by Seren in 2015 and won the Geoffrey Faber Memorial Prize. She won a Northern Writers Award (2014), an Eric Gregory Award (2011) and the Geoffrey Dearmer Prize (2010). She is currently a PhD student at Manchester Metropolitan University. Kim's poem 'My Sister and the Wolves' won third prize in the Bristol Poetry Prize 2016.

Helen Mort has published two poetry collections with Chatto & Windus. Her first novel, *Black Car Burning*, will be published in early 2019.

Abi Palmer is an interactive artist & writer. Her current project 'Sanatorium' explores language, rehabilitation and movement in and out of water. She wrote 'No Body to Write With: Intrusion as a Manifesto for D/deaf and Disabled Writers' for *Stairs and Whispers: D/deaf and Disabled Poets Write Back* (Nine Arches Press). www.abipalmer.com

Amerah Saleh is a British Yemeni poet from Birmingham. She has been writing and performing spoken word and theatre for 10 years. She is a board member at Birmingham Repertory Theatre and a Producer at

Free Radical - part of the Beatfreeks collective. Amerah's poem 'Naeema' was first published in Amerah's debut collection, *I Am Not From Here*, through new Birmingham Indie, Verve Poetry Press in 2018.

Giles Turnbull is a blind poet living in south Wales. His poetry and articles have appeared in several magazines and anthologies. He was shortlisted in the Bridport poetry prize in 2017 and his debut pamphlet, *Dressing Up*, is published by Cinnamon Press.

Lizzy Turner is a poet living in Bristol, though her heart belongs to South London. She co-edits the Lunar Poetry Podcast, and produces its companion podcast A Poem A Week. She has co-edited *'Why Poetry?'* - *The Lunar Poetry Podcasts Anthology*. Her work appears in various publications online and in print.

Jane Yeh is the author of *The Ninjas* (2012) and *Marabou* (2005), both published by Carcanet. Her next collection is forthcoming in 2019. Jane's poem 'A Short History of Violence' originally appeared in the anthology, *tremble: The University of Canberra Vice-Chancellor's International Poetry Prize 2016*.

ACKNOWLEDGEMENTS

Firstly, thank you to all the poets in this book who have been very generous with their time and work. I am hugely grateful to Verve Poetry Press for offering me and Lizzy the chance to look back over four years of Lunar Poetry Podcasts. It has been wonderful (and at times hugely embarrassing!) to revisit the archive. I can't believe we now have a book. But it's there. Look! In your hands.

A huge thank-you to the guest-hosts, all of whom have played vital and significant roles in making the series what it is. In order of appearance those wonderful humans are: Paul McMenemy, Lizzy Turner, Kyla Manenti, Michelle Madsen, Jacob Sam-La Rose, Paula Varjack, The Repeat Beat Poet, Harry Josephine Giles, Emily Harrison, Melissa Lee-Houghton, Rachel Long and Khairani Barokka. The role of Paul McMenemy is particularly important; had he not invited me to write reviews of spoken word events, back in 2014, for his fantastic Lunar Poetry Magazine, this series would never have existed.

I continue to be overwhelmed by the generosity and support of several organisations, especially Spread the Word, Speaking Volumes, Poetry Translation Centre, The Poetry Exchange and, of course, Arts Council England. LPP would never have reached this point without Helen Zaltzman's Facebook group Podcasters' Support Group and the advice of individuals like Sarah Sanders, Matt Hill...

...and Abi Palmer. Abi is a constant source of inspiration. I'm so grateful to her for removing from me the burden of writing an introduction to this book and turning it into a fun and often very emotional conversation. It couldn't be more fitting.

Most importantly, a dizzying pile of thank-yous and love hearts scribbled on miniature Post-It notes for my wonderful wife Lizzy. As co-editor of LPP and editor of her own series a poem a week, it's impossible to put into words how much she has added to the project. Without her not much would be possible, especially this series. Her support and patience has kept this [noun] [verb]. I'm incredibly lucky and grateful to share my life with a person that shares my passion for words and the right of everyone to have a voice.

Finally, thank you to everyone that has downloaded/listened to/shared an episode. It's been an absolute pleasure to bring these (230+) poets to you. I've loved talking to you.

David xx

ALSO AVAILABLE FROM VERVE POETRY PRESS

It All Radiates Outwards:
The Verve Anthology Of City Poems

Curated and introduced by Luke Kennard.

This book contains the winning and commended poems from the Verve Festival 2018 City Themed Poetry Competition judged by Luke Kennard. They are the best of an extremely good bunch of poems that we received on the subject – from all over the country, but also from Europe, the USA, Africa and The Middle East. The book includes winning poems from C.I.Marshall, Jacqueline Saphra, Claire Trevien, as well as Polly Atkin, Sarah Cave, and David Turner.

Alongside these poems you will find six city poems that Verve commissioned from our own selection of local poets of note in Birmingham: Roy McFarlane, Bohdan Piasecki, Amerah Saleh, Jenna Clake, Casey Bailey and Ahlaam Moledina.

Taken together, the poems show cities in all their giddy, tortuous variety and from every conceivable angle. The forms and styles chosen to tackle this subject are as diverse as the city itself. The clamour and the noise is deafening. Make this anthology your next city destination!

ISBN: 978 1 912565 03 0
84 pages • 216 x 138 • 32 poems
£9.99

ABOUT VERVE POETRY PRESS

Verve Poetry Press is a new press focussing initially on meeting a local need in Birmingham - a need for the vibrant poetry scene here in Brum to find a way to present itself to the poetry world via publication. Co-founded by Stuart Bartholomew and Amerah Saleh, it will be publishing poets this year from all corners of the city - poets that represent the city's varied and energetic qualities and will communicate its many poetic stories. Look out in 2018 for stunning first collections from Amerah, Casey Bailey, Leon Priestnall, Nafeesa Hamid, Rupinder Kaur and Hannah Swings.

We will also look to help poets/producers from further afield who have supported or featured at Verve Poetry Festival and who we feel it is important to get into print. Lunar Poetry Podcasts falls into this category. They are part of the Verve family hving appeared at both festivals, first recording and then delivering live interviews. It is a pleasure to help them celebrate four incredible years with this wonderful anthology.

Like the festival, our press will strive to think about poetry in inclusive ways and embrace the multiplicity of approaches towards this glorious art.

Keep an eye on what we are up to! Sign up to our mailing list at https://vervepoetrypress.com/mailing-list

https://vervepoetrypress.com
@VervePoetryPres
mail@vervepoetrypress.com